THE
Archive Photographs
SERIES

WESTMINSTER'S
VILLAGES

Costermonger, Trafalgar Square, *c.* 1912.

THE
Archive Photographs
SERIES

WESTMINSTER'S VILLAGES

Compiled by
Brian Girling

CHALFORD

First published 1996
Copyright © Brian Girling, 1996

The Chalford Publishing Company
St Mary's Mill, Chalford,
Stroud, Gloucestershire, GL6 8NX

ISBN 0 7524 0683 3

Typesetting and origination by
The Chalford Publishing Company
Printed in Great Britain by
Redwood Books, Trowbridge

Shepherd Market, *c.* 1905.

Contents

Moreton Street, Pimlico, *c.* 1906.

Acknowledgements

A book like this is richer for the contributions and help of others,
for which a big 'thank you' is due to the
Greater London Record Office,
Judges of Hastings (01424 420919),
Westminster Archive Centre, and David Brewster.

Introduction

London has often been likened to a collection of villages – a vast conglomeration of neighbourhoods, each with its own character and style. Some of the features of the English village have their urban equivalents in the capital city, and at its centre, Westminster, it is still possible to see an old fashioned fun fair on the cobblestones of Covent Garden, a garden fete in Deans Yard beside Westminster School, an open air party in the stuccoed streets of Belgravia, maypole dancing on the ancient lawns of Westminster Abbey, and a horse drawn wagon gathering harvested hay in royal Hyde Park.

Using rare, previously unpublished photographs, this book explores some of the villages and neighbourhoods of Westminster, a city famed worldwide for its history, royal residences and traditions, military pageantry, theatres, art galleries and shops. Within a few paces of some of this country's greatest treasures is the Londoner's own Westminster, with a collection of neighbourhoods as diverse as any in London.

The most populous of them is Pimlico, which was developed during the 1830s from a neglected Thames-side area of marshy land and scattered cottages, once known as The Neathouses. Much of this desolate landscape between Belgravia, Chelsea, and Vauxhall Bridge Road was acquired by the builder, Thomas Cubitt, who set about transforming it into a new residential area. The style of the new terraces of tall town houses mirrored that of Cubitt's earlier developments in Belgravia. After the Second World War, the southern area had become badly run down, but the 1950s saw the beginning of a vast programme of redevelopment with bright modern municipal housing, while the surviving terraces of Cubitt's Pimlico emerged from post-war dowdiness with bright new paint, to become the attractive inner city area we know today.

The area familiar to us as Belgravia once had a notorious reputation as a haunt of footpads and highwaymen, who infested the barren grazing lands of Five Fields to such an extent that a crossing of the Westbourne stream earned itself the name 'Bloody Bridge'. Eventually, the fields were used as market gardens before Thomas Cubitt and others acquired building rights from the Grosvenor Estate during the 1820s, transforming the area into a spacious and fashionable quarter of nineteenth-century London, conveniently close to Buckingham Palace.

Knightsbridge was once the first village out of London on the road to Kensington, deriving its name from the presence of a bridge over the Westbourne near what is now Albert Gate. It, too, became fashionable but something of the rural past still seems to linger in the cobbled mews and old-fashioned by-ways, with their coachman's pubs that lay behind the opulent department stores and grand hotels.

Lordly Mayfair is older than Belgravia, and even more aristocratic. However, at its heart, the eighteenth-century Shepherd Market, built on fields in an effort to disrupt the holding of a riotous annual May fair, still delights, with its narrow pedestrian passages, old shops and, more recently, smart pavement cafes and restaurants.

St James's is older still, a seventeenth-century expansion of Westminster that has become the traditional home of West End gentleman's clubs and numerous fine art galleries, all in close proximity to King Henry VIII's St James Palace.

Soho, on the other hand, is a very different place, a highly cosmopolitan quarter since the seventeenth century when French Protestant refugees (the Huguenots), and other foreign immigrants made their homes in the dense maze of new but narrow streets. The multi-national community has enriched London with the sometimes exotic nature of its shopping streets, where the days never seem to end. A heady mix of foreign restaurants, delicatessens, theatres and old family businesses can be found alongside a latterday Chinatown that could have been lifted straight out of an oriental city. Crowded pavement cafes and grid-locked traffic contribute to the ambience, together with the more lurid neon-lit attractions of Soho's traditional 'continental' book shops, night-clubs and 'models'.

One of London's most famous places, Piccadilly Circus, was carved out of narrow Soho streets during the last century, and has shone an electronic welcome to the world throughout the present one. 'Theatreland' is part of it all, spreading eastwards through the old market district of Covent Garden to Aldwych and Kingsway, two early-twentieth-century streets, whose construction also led to the demise of old neighbourhoods, including the bookseller's quarter of Holywell Street.

Westminster is a constantly evolving city, and nowhere is this more apparent than in the Millbank/Horseferry Road area, where the reeking damp-plagued slums of the Edwardian era have given way to a proud modern cityscape. To the north of this greatly regenerated district lies the historic heart of Westminster where, over 1,000 years ago, the great Abbey of Westminster and its predecessors arose on the bramble infested Thorney Island and where, centuries later, evidence of Iron Age and Roman occupation was to be discovered. The adjoining Palace of Westminster was a royal residence from the time of the Danish King, Canute, to that of Henry VIII and the meeting place of the earliest English parliament during the thirteenth century.

Further along the Thames, another triumph of Victorian engineering gave London the riverside splendour of Victoria Embankment on land reclaimed from the Thames, effectively divorcing riverside mansions and communities from the waters that had, for centuries, lapped their walls.

The historic images that illustrate the story of Westminster during the last ninety years and more will hopefully evoke a sense of nostalgia among the city's older residents, and also interest the many visitors from every corner of the world who come to explore the wonders that Westminster has to offer.

Photographic reproductions of many of the pictures are available from the author, telephone 0181 8639194.

Refreshment Kiosk ('The Tin Cow'), by Horse Guards Parade, St James's Park, c. 1905.

One

Pimlico

LONDON.   Warwick Street, S. W.   No. 1757

Warwick Street from Vauxhall Bridge Road, *c.* 1920. A hole in the ground illuminated by a pair of hurricane lamps temporarily displaces one of the Warwick Street's fruit stalls in this bustling Pimlico market. The street market was established here during the 1860s, before moving to its present location in Tachbrook Street. Some of the modest Victorian shops on the right still stand, but the Duchess of Clarence pub on the right was rebuilt in 1927. The Queens Arms, now the Slug & Lettuce, can be seen on the Tachbrook Street corner. The road has been slightly widened and the flats and shops of George Eliot House have replaced those at the left of the view. Warwick Street was renamed Warwick Way during the 1930s.

A panorama of southern Westminster and Pimlico from the campanile of Westminster Cathedral, *c.* 1910. The most prominent feature is Vincent Square, one of London's largest garden squares, whose grassy acres are now used as playing fields by Westminster School. The road running from left to right in front of Vincent Square is Rochester Row, where the pointed gable of its police station may be seen. A gas-holder of the former Chartered Gas Works is seen behind the house and flats of Regency Street (left), and the terraces of the now rebuilt Lillington Street area are beyond Vauxhall Bridge Road to the right. The photograph pre-dated the arrival of the ubiquitous tower blocks, and the church towers which still stood out high above the roof tops included those of: Holy Trinity, Bessborough Gardens (now demolished); St James-the-Less, Thorndike Street; and St Gabriel's, Warwick Square. There were few undeveloped sites in Westminster early in the twentieth century, but a large one is revealed, bottom right, with allotments and gardens flourishing where Victoria telephone exchange was later built. The distant horizon at Sydenham shows a famous building that once stood in Westminster, Crystal Palace. This mighty glass and iron structure was designed by Sir Joseph Paxton for the Great International Exhibition of 1851 in Hyde Park. Following the closure of the exhibition, the Crystal Palace was dismantled and rebuilt at Sydenham where it stood until its spectacular destruction by fire on the night of 30 November 1936, an inferno visible from all over London.

The Grosvenor canal, *c.* 1906. The surviving stretch of the Grosvenor canal is one of the last remnants of a commercial Pimlico riverfront which once contained numerous wharves and docks. The waterway was begun in 1725 by the Chelsea Waterworks Company, and was reconstructed by the Grosvenor Estate during the early 1820s, its curving route taking it from the Thames to a large terminal basin on the site of what is now part of Victoria Station. The canal ran behind Buckingham Palace Road (previously Chelsea Road), and wharves still lined the southern part of that road early in this century. When the Victoria (Grosvenor) bridge, London's first Thames railway bridge, opened in 1860, it carried the London, Brighton and South Coast Railway into Pimlico, the track running beside the canal to a new wooden Victoria station. The Grosvenor Hotel was also built on part of the canal basin, and opened in 1861. This view looks from Grosvenor Road, and shows the lock gates, with the timber yards of Knight & Sons, by Gatliff and Lock wharves. Ebury Bridge, once a wooden canal bridge, is in the background. The short surviving fragment of the Grosvenor canal still performs a useful service for London, with a terminal for the container barges that take some of the city's domestic refuse from the City of Westminster's waste transfer station downstream to landfill sites near the Thames estuary.

They called it 'Commercial Road', which was once an accurate reflection of the road's image with its saw-mills and wharves backing on to the Grosvenor canal. Most of the canal was eventually filled in, and by the end of the 1930s, the road had taken on a more residential aspect with new blocks of flats and a more attractive name, Ebury Bridge Road. The shops in this view from around 1906 included a stationer, bootmaker and greengrocer. Further along was the long vanished Robert Street with the William IV pub, presided over by landlady Mrs Amelia Mazdon. Gatliff Road (right) still exists and leads to Westminster's waste transfer station on the surviving section of Grosvenor canal. The site of the shops was taken by James House, an office block.

Wellington Buildings, c. 1906. The arrival of an Edwardian photographer with his mahogany and brass camera on its stand was always an attraction for the local youth who have turned out here in force to make sure of a place in this portrayal of the impressive Victorian Wellington Buildings, off Commercial Road (Ebury Bridge Road).

All Saints church and Thames Parade, Grosvenor Road, *c*. 1910. Thames Parade survives as a rare Victorian interlude in the midst of this area's postwar modernity, but All Saints church, built in 1871, was demolished in 1974. The William IV pub, left, still flourishes on the corner of what used to be Glasgow Terrace.

Glasgow Terrace from Grosvenor Road, *c*. 1930. Glasgow Terrace lost all its original housing with the creation of the Churchill Gardens estate, the vast post-war redevelopment of southern Pimlico, the first part of which was opened by the Duchess of Marlborough on 24 March 1951. The estate was completed in 1962 and contains over 1,600 homes. The view shows one of the estate's few surviving early buildings, the Victorian St Gabriel's Church of England School, which now stands beside the estate's principal thoroughfare, Churchill Gardens Road.

Lupus Street, c. 1920. The western end of Lupus Street now marks the dividing line between Churchill Gardens Estate and the network of Victorian roads to the north where the old street pattern is retained. Here, on the south side of Lupus Street, all the shops were replaced by the newer facilities of Churchill Gardens, including the branch of Walton, Hassell & Port, the grocers. This was once a familiar high street name, and there were two branches in Lupus Street. Their neighbour was the British Meat Co., with the Gun Tavern beyond at the Glasgow Terrace corner. The spire of St Saviour's church can be seen in the distance.

The Balmoral Castle, Glamorgan Street, c. 1928. A jolly party finds a moment for an official photograph before setting off an a charabanc trip, probably to the races. The pub still stands, but its old neighbourhood has been replaced by the grass, trees, and flats of Churchill Gardens.

14

Rutland Street, *c.* 1906. After the Second World War, the tightly packed streets of southern Pimlico gave way to the bright modern flats of Churchill Gardens leaving little trace of the former neighbourhoods. Rutland Street (Antrobus Street from the 1930s) once overlooked a long vanished waterway, Belgrave Dock, which was entered from the Thames under a bridge at Grosvenor Road. Belgrave Dock was beyond the fence to the right of this view.

Ranelagh Road from Lupus Street, *c.* 1920. Ranelagh Road still exists but only at the Lupus Street end, where nine of the houses on the left survive, as does the school on the right. The view shows Taylor's furniture repository, here for over 100 years at premises backing onto the waters of Belgrave Dock.

Charlwood Street from Lupus Street, *c.* 1920. Walter Mingard's stationery shop also accommodated Charlwood Street post office in a building that has since reverted to private housing. The shops on the left still stand, but the houses beyond them have been replaced by the flats of Russell House.

The Army Clothing Depot, Grosvenor Road, *c.* 1905. Only a small part of this seven-acre complex, which once employed 700 people, is visible here. It occupied the site of the building yard established in 1839 by Thomas Cubitt for his new Pimlico housing projects. Its replacement in 1937, by Dolphin Square, gave Pimlico one of Europe's largest self-contained blocks of flats, with over 1,200 flats, shops, and a restaurant. Part of St George's Square can be seen at the right.

Warwick Street (Warwick Way), *c.* 1905. Warwick Street was as popular with local shoppers at the beginning of the century as it remains at the end of it. Here we see a lively scene in the market by Hindon Street (now Wilton Road), with full-skirted Edwardian ladies and a postman with an empty sack, having completed his round. The terrace on the right was dominated by the drapery stores of Henry Howells, and E.W. Rose & Co., with the dental surgery of Edward Bird to the left. In those pre-national health service days, Mr Bird would have removed a troublesome molar for 2/6d (12½p).

A view of Churton Street from around 1908 when its shops extended as far as Vauxhall Bridge Road. Although the block on the left, then with Charles Painter's newsagents shop on the corner, still stands, the rest have been swept away with the building of another post-war estate, Lillington Gardens. The intersection with Tachbrook Street can be seen here, with John Guyer's provision shop on one corner and Mrs Elizabeth Titswell's toy shop on the other. Her shop offered a fascinating selection of steam driven models, magic lanterns and 'choice dolls'.

Tachbrook Street from Charlwood Street, *c.* 1905. Following the Second World War, this street presented a run-down appearance to the world, but as Pimlico's fortunes revived, the houses on the right were restored, and those on the left replaced with Westminster Council's attractively leafy Lillington Gardens Estate. The view shows the Enterprise wine stores on the Charlwood Street corner where 'wines from the wood' could be obtained from 3d (about 1½p) 'per large dock glass'. The corner is now occupied by a new pub, with a name that revives memories of long-lost local transport, The Pimlico Tram.

Jenks' Stores, Tachbrook Street, *c.* 1906. Harry Jenks and his staff pose outside their 'Oil and Italian' store on the Charlwood Street corner. This was a useful shop for the local community, with a vast range of household goods, and a 'travelling oil store' for local deliveries. The shop was licenced to sell 'Benzoline Methylated and Motor Spirits', and a gallon of Shell or Pratts Motor Spirit would have been delivered to the door for 1/- (5p). Very little daylight could have penetrated the crowded window display.

18

Lillington Street from Moreton Street, c. 1908. Nothing remains of this populous street other than the name which lives on in Lillington Gardens, the attractive municipal housing scheme that replaced the old terraces during the 1960s and 1970s. In 1908, a second floor room in Lillington Street could have been rented for 7/- (35p) per week.

Chimney sweep, Lillington Street, c. 1905. In the days when everyone had a coal fire, a clean chimney was essential to maintain the updraught necessary to keep the fire burning well. A build up of soot happened all too frequently – the fire would fill the room with acrid smoke and it was time for the ritual of a visit from the sweep! This was nothing to be taken lightly, as breakables and soft furnishings would have to moved out of harms way, and everything protected with dust sheets from the soot-blackened gentleman with his poles and brushes. Messrs Phillips & Lewis of 119 Lillington Street conveyed their equipment by tricycle that informed of their appointment as chimney sweeps to the London County Council.

Vauxhall Bridge, 1906. The first Vauxhall Bridge, originally called The Regent's Bridge, opened in 1816 and was replaced by the present structure in 1906. The view is from Grosvenor Road and shows the bridge when it was brand new during the brief period from 26 May to 5 August 1906 when horse-drawn trams ran over the bridge prior to electrification of the route. The horse-trams connected the stations at Victoria and Vauxhall.

Vauxhall Bridge, c. 1907. The reign of the horse-tram on Vauxhall Bridge was a short one, and from 5 August 1906 the new electric trams provided a more efficient service and a connection with the vast south London tramway network. The bright new tramcars, ablaze with electric light after dark, brought a breath of the latest twentieth-century technology to streets still thronged with the nineteenth century's legacy of horse-drawn traffic. This view looks from Vauxhall to Pimlico, where the elegant spire of Holy Trinity church, Bessborough Gardens (built 1849-51, demolished 1951) can be seen above the wharves of Grosvenor Road.

Vauxhall Bridge Road by Regency Street, *c.* 1920. The road, like the original bridge, dates from 1816, when it rapidly gained popularity as a route between Westminster and south London. The tram in the centre of the photograph was working route 58, Victoria to Forest Hill and Catford, while the open top bus, a 'B' type owned by London General Omnibus Company (forerunners of London Transport), was running on route 36a to Grove Park. The musical hits of the day could be obtained at Henry Roberts' record and phonograph shop on the Regency Street corner (right).

Regency Street from Vauxhall Bridge Road, *c.* 1920. Modest terrace houses still stood in Regency Street during the 1920s, but these were rather overshadowed by the newer Metropolitan Police section house. One penny ice-creams were among the temptations offered at the tobacconist's shop by Douglas Street, left, where a modern office block now stands.

Vauxhall Bridge Road by Chapter Street, *c.* 1907. This was not the most peaceful place to live following the arrival of the heavy electric trams whose vibrations would shake the houses as they passed by. The crash of heavy iron shod wagon wheels, as they negotiated the tram lines, added to the din. The photograph shows a typically busy scene in this well used road with a delivery of forage in progress at the shop of Frederick Lilley, the corn dealer, left.

Vauxhall Bridge Road from Charlwood Street, *c.* 1905. The old terraces on the left, including the shop of Lomath Bros., furniture removers, and Benjamin Hollaway's shampooing saloon are a distant memory, but the Surprise pub can still be found on the corner of Stanford Street. The long monotonous row of houses on the right was another to be replaced by the extensive Lillington Gardens Estate.

Victory Parade, Vauxhall Bridge Road, 19 July 1919. The weary years of the First World War finally came to an end, and it was time for the nation to celebrate with a great victory parade through the streets of London. As ever, Londoners love a free show and turned out in force to view the spectacle, thronging the streets and windows. Even rooftops were crowded as spectators secured a variety of precarious viewpoints among Pimlico's chimney pots. A view from Parnell's department store at the Victoria end of Vauxhall Bridge Road as the crowds gather to watch the parade. Gillingham Street is on the right.

The view towards Victoria as the military bands march past. Even the roof of the Victoria Palace theatre (far distance), was crowded with spectators.

The Victoria Picture Palace, Vauxhall Bridge Road, *c.* 1911. This photograph shows one of Westminster's famous centres of entertainment during its earliest manifestation. The Victoria Picture Palace opened around 1910 with a 498-seat auditorium in a modest conversion of the lower floors of two nineteenth-century terraced houses. The cinema, which also had an entrance from Wilton Road, lasted until 1926, when demolition of the whole block made way for one of London's most dramatic and innovative super-cinemas, the 2,786-seat New Victoria, which opened on 15 October 1930. The building was spectacular by any standards, with its exotic decoration and artful lighting that likened the auditorium to an immense fantasy palace beneath the sea, including illuminated stalactites and art-deco designs. London's taxi drivers, never short of an opinion, were less impressed with the New Victoria's sleek exterior and likened it to 'a prison'. The cinema closed for business on 1 November 1975, but re-opened as a theatre, the Apollo Victoria, on 15 September 1980, specialising in musical stage shows and pop concerts. Sir Andrew Lloyd-Webber's *Starlight Express* opened here in 1984 where it remains to this day. The centre of the photograph shows the much loved clock tower 'Little Ben' beyond Victoria's tram terminus. 'Little Ben' was erected in 1892, and after a long absence for restoration has been re-erected at its old location. The trams ceased running here in 1952.

Wilton Road from Gillingham Street, *c.* 1912. The row of tiny shops next to the Fountain pub (right) contained the entrance to another early cinema, the Electric Theatre, more familiar in later years as the Biograph. The cinema opened on 24 May 1909 and seated 560 patrons in an auditorium behind the shops. Closure on 4 August 1983 was followed two days later by demolition for the site's use as a car park, a role it still fulfils. The terrace further along has been replaced by a high-rise office block with a new road running beneath it called Neathouse Place, a name that recalls Pimlico's earliest days.

Gillingham Street from Wilton Road, *c.* 1905. This was a residential street in Edwardian days, but shops have taken over the ground floors now. Joseph Conrad, the novelist, once occupied number 17. Candy & Candy's Victoria wine stores was on the corner of Hindon Street, the old name for the southern part of Wilton Road. An advertising board tempts the passerby with 'cheap trains to Brighton and back' for 3/- (15p), from Victoria station.

Hindon Street (Wilton Road), 1906. 'This shows you our new motor buses going down Hindon Street from Victoria. I thought it might please you to see a little bit of home', writes the sender of this postcard during October 1906 to a Pimlico exile living in New Zealand. These Milnes-Daimler buses were the last word in modernity in 1906. This one ran to St John's Wood and Childs Hill but, as was the custom at that time, it did not display a route number.

Hindon Street (Wilton Road), c. 1906. More of Hindon Street's shops, with William John's piano shop at No. 42, and Meaker Bros. the outfitters, next door, with a fine array of straw boaters in their window. St Leonard's Street, now called Longmoore Street, can be seen (centre) where some of these old properties still stand.

The Monster Tavern, Sutherland Terrace, 1907. This famous pub, a Victorian rebuild of an earlier inn and tea garden, stood at the corner of Sutherland Terrace and Winchester Street until its untimely demise during an air raid on 11 April 1941. The flats of Sherborne House stand here now. The Monster was also an early bus terminus, and a popular one with drivers. Here we see a gathering of five horse-drawn buses, one of which carried an advertisement for the Austrian Exhibition, held at Earls Court in 1907.

Sutherland Terrace, c. 1906. This was a large block of shops that formerly stood at the Sutherland Street/Sutherland Terrace junction, and where Arthur Mardon's drapery store occupied a commanding corner position. The photographer was standing near Ebury Bridge from where the same viewpoint now reveals the post-war municipal flats of the Abbots Manor Estate.

Warwick Street (Warwick Way), c. 1905. Following war-time destruction, the Abbots Manor Estate has utilised the site of all these houses and the Kings Head pub on the Sutherland Street corner. The view is from Ebury Bridge, whose fly-posted brickwork is seen on the left, with Hugh Street beyond, where the high-rise block of Glastonbury House now stands.

Pimlico Road and Ranelagh Grove, c. 1905. It was sale time at Mrs Sarah Lambert's pair of furniture shops at Nos 7 and 9 Pimlico Road, where the stock included a range of prams, carpets and 'mail carts'. Everything was displayed in the typically cluttered style of the Edwardian era, with stock piled up on the pavement, and baby carriages parked at the kerb-side. The shop was founded in 1876 and closed early in this century.

Pimlico Road from Buckingham Palace Road, c. 1905. The shops on the left curved round into Ranelagh Grove and then included a branch of the popular grocery chain, Oakeshotts Ltd. These vanished long ago, as did the shops on the right where the pre-war flats of Fountain Court and Walden House now stand. A mixture of road users here included a donkey drawn cart, a tricycle delivery cart, and a horse-bus bound for Hyde Park Corner.

Pimlico Road from Avery Farm Row, c. 1906. The Union pub, now the Ebury Arms, still stands on the Ranelagh Grove corner, but the shops from Avery Farm Row to Cliffords Row were replaced by flats during the 1930s. The spire of St Barnabas church is seen above the rooftops.

West Street by Ranelagh Grove, c. 1906. This street runs from Ebury Bridge Road to Ranelagh Grove, and was renamed St Barnabas Street during the 1930s. Its terraces of typically London style cottages have been beautifully preserved, but the General Havelock pub was rebuilt in a modern version of a Georgian style. The view shows a delivery wagon of the Cannon Brewery Company of Clerkenwell.

St Barnabas church from Ebury Street, c. 1906. The atmosphere of a London village survives strongly here, with local shops overlooking a leafy triangular open space created at the junction of Pimlico Road with Ebury Street. Much of the roadway seen here has been pedestrianised, adding to the 'village green', which has been given the name 'Orange Square' after the Orange theatre which once stood nearby. A statue of Mozart, who once lived in Ebury Street, was unveiled here by Princess Margaret on 21 March 1994. The scene is still presided over by the church of St Barnabas, which was built from 1847 to 1850 to designs by Thomas Cundy jr., and Willaim Butterfield. The roadway shows some of the wood block paving that was once commonplace in London.

Coleshill Buildings, Pimlico Road, c. 1905. These flats were built by the Improved Industrial Dwellings Company during the early 1870s and can still be seen today. John Harwood & Sons antique shop (left), was a forerunner of those that flourish here today, while further along, older shops can be seen jutting out at the corner of a long lost side turning, Cliffords Row. Pimlico Road had a few market stalls, one of which is seen on the right selling flowers. St Barnabas School is on the right.

Pimlico Road, c. 1915. This is the Ebury Street junction, with some of the market stalls and barrows that gathered in front of the former chapel of St John the Baptist, whose site has since been filled with shops. During the early part of the nineteenth century, this part of Pimlico Road was known as Grosvenor Row, while its eastern end was called Queen Street.

Pimlico Road by Bloomfield Place, *c.* 1906. Benjamin Bosher's pawnshop stood on the corner, with Alf Cooke's 'Guards Boot Depot' next door, where a new pair of men's boots would have cost 5/11d (just under 30p).

Pimlico Road, *c.* 1906. The shop of Frederick Thornhill, the corn, seed and hay merchant occupied the corner of Union Street, a side turning that acquired a new name, Passmore Street, in the 1930s. The Misses Emma, Maria and Alice Gayler, the linen drapers, traded from an attractive pair of shops next to Thornhill's. Note the rather unusual double kerbstones.

Two
Belgravia
and Knightsbridge

West Halkin Street from Lowndes Street, c. 1905. Despite the stuccoed splendour of its nineteenth-century squares, terraces and crescents, there remains today a strong sense of a London village to be found in Belgravia, particularly in the leafy cobble-stoned mews, and pretty streets of small exclusive shops and restaurants that lie behind the great architectural set pieces. West Halkin Street is a beautifully preserved thoroughfare, dating from around 1830, and apart from the traffic, appears little changed since Edwardian days. The shops, of course, have newer occupants, and today, an up-market antiques gallery may be found in place of Lovegrove & Flint's stationery shop on the Lowndes Street corner. Further along, the tiny Belgrave Presbyterian church can seen, still fulfiling its religious role, before conversion into a most unusual eight bedroomed private house. In later years, this was adapted as an exclusive eating club, the Belfry, where members could dine in gothic splendour. The Belfry was later acquired by Swiss chef Anton Mosimann in whose hands it now flourishes as 'Mosimann's Belfry'.

Ebury Street from Pimlico Road, *c.* 1905. Pimlico merges into Belgravia at Ebury Street, a long road that extends northeastwards, almost to Buckingham Palace. Beyond the Wyatt family's trio of shops (left), is a row of eighteenth-century houses, one of which accommodated the boy genius Mozart who, together with his father, Leopold, would have enjoyed a rural outlook from their windows, for the houses, then called Five Fields Row, were the first to be built here. To the right, beyond the bulk of Coleshill Flats, was a terrace of houses by Ebury Square that was destroyed during the Second World War, and replaced by Cundy Street Flats.

Ebury Square, *c.* 1905. This tiny square was built in 1820 on land that was once part of Ebury Farm. Residents of the plain brick houses would have appreciated their view of the leafy garden with its fountain and flower beds, but, although the square remains a green oasis, the houses have been replaced by part of Cundy Street Flats, and the modern Semley and Johnson Houses.

Jacob Hexamer's bakery stood on the Eaton Terrace corner, and is seen here with handcarts piled with loaves in readiness for the local delivery. The bakery windows bear a name still familiar to us, 'Hovis', a company that had flour mills by Vauxhall Bridge and on Millbank. The whole block, including the distant Red Lion pub has been rebuilt with high modern flats, Kilmuir House.

Ebury Street by Eccleston Street, *c.* 1920. A motorist speeds towards the Eccleston Street junction in the enviably peaceful road conditions of the early 1920s, while two ladies enjoy their chat as they stroll past Thomas Rastall's stationery shop (right). A house towards the centre of this view was once occupied by Ian Fleming, creator of 'James Bond'.

Ebury Street, *c.* 1906. These houses, and the Sun pub, are seen in the last years of their lives before giving way in 1910 to a smart new arrival, the Goring Hotel. It takes its name from O.R. Goring, the proprietor, and claimed to be the first hotel in the world to have a bathroom and central heating to every bedroom. This eastern part of Ebury Street is now called Beeston Place.

Westbourne Street from Ebury Street, c. 1906. This street was renamed Bourne Street during the 1930s, and appears little changed in ninety years, although many of the houses have been rebuilt or refurbished and are now highly sought after properties. The name 'Westbourne' comes from the stream of that name, which flows underground for most of its length, apart from one glorious stretch where its waters have been dammed to create the Serpentine in Kensington Gardens and Hyde Park, (see page 51).

Gerald Road, c. 1906. This is one of Belgravia's more attractive smaller streets, with its early-nineteenth-century town houses. Those beyond the now closed Gerald Road police station are rather unusual for the area, with front gardens instead of the open basements and railings which are more usually found.

Elizabeth Street, *c.* 1905. A carriage and coachman waits by Gerald Road in an Edwardian scene typical of this wealthy quarter of town. To the right, the shop of Henry Dawe, the shirtmaker, also accommodated Elizabeth Street post office, with L. de Vere's Belgravia Dress Agency next door. The Prince of Wales pub still stands on the Ebury Mews corner.

Ye Royal Oak, Elizabeth Street, *c.* 1906. Landlord George Gale stands with some of his clients at the door of this long vanished pub, which stood at the northwestern extremity of Elizabeth Street, beside Royal Oak Place, a side turning more familiar now as Boscobel Place. A modern block of flats has replaced the pub.

Chester Terrace, (Chester Row), *c.* 1906. This fashionable street looks rather gloomy here when it still had a pair of shops, those of William Lakeman, florist, and Messrs Jones & Betts, builders and decorators. Their buildings still stand, but are now private houses.

St Michael's church, Chester Square, from Elizabeth Street, *c.* 1904. St Michael's dates from 1846, and was designed by Thomas Cundy jr., but it was enlarged by the addition of a War Memorial chapel in 1920, designed by Sir Giles Gilbert Scott. This is noticeable from the outside, having been finished in a different stone to the rest of the church. The sooty London atmosphere had blackened the original ragstone masonry when photographed here, but a clean-up in recent years has restored the stonework to pristine condition.

Eaton Terrace, *c.* 1906. Eaton Terrace post office on the Caroline Street (now Caroline Terrace) corner doubled as another branch of Jacob Hexamer's bakery, while the first floor accommodated Ellen Smith's 'Modes and Robes'. The Eaton place names hereabouts come from Eaton Hall, Cheshire, seat of the landowners, the Grosvenor family, Dukes of Westminster.

Eaton chapel, *c.* 1905. This early-nineteenth-century chapel stood at the Eaton Terrace/Eaton Gate corner until its replacement early in the twentieth century by an impressive group of town houses, built to designs by Messr Balfour and Turner.

Lower Belgrave Street from Ebury Street, *c.* 1905. This is another of Belgravia's smart residential and shopping streets, which, apart from the shop fronts, has changed little in ninety years.

Eaton Square, *c.* 1904. Some of the most spectacular of Belgravia's domestic architecture may be seen at Eaton Square, in a display that almost rivals that of the Nash terraces in Regents Park. Here we see the northern side of this elongated 'square', with its remarkable colonades on terraces built to Thomas Cubitt's designs at the end of the 1820s. Eaton Square is divided by Kings Road, originally 'The Kings Private Road', which was used by King Charles II on his journeys from London to Hampton Court Palace, through what was then open countryside.

Wilton Crescent from Motcomb Street, *c.* 1905. The houses were built by W.H. Seth-Smith in 1827, but their appearance altered dramatically early in the twentieth century, when they were refaced in stone, giving a street scene more akin to Bath than London.

Motcomb Street, *c.* 1905. Motcomb Street was laid out in 1830, and remains a wonderfully preserved example of an early-nineteenth-century shopping street in the village heart of Belgravia. The great Doric colonnade on the left fronted the Pantechnicon, a labyrinthine construction of wine vaults, carriage houses, and warehouses, advertised as 'fireproof', until February 1874 when it burnt down. Mercifully, the façade resisted the flames and stands today adding dignity to this charming street. The two shops on the left proudly display their Royal Warrants; the wine merchant Charles Forder on the left, with the Irish Linen Industries Association, which supplied Irish linen 'direct from the workers' next door.

Wilton Crescent, c. 1905. The eastern section of Wilton Crescent was also refaced in stone, giving the whole a nobler, more unified appearance. Past residents included no less than nine MPs in 1854, and Algernon Swinburne, the poet, who lived here in 1856.

Kinnerton Street from Motcomb Street, c. 1905. By Belgravia's standards, this was a very modest byway, with its small shops, coachman's pubs, and stables. Everything in this view has been replaced in recent times, but at the Knightsbridge end of Kinnerton Street, the tiny courts, passageways, cottages, and one of London's smallest pubs have survived in a picturesque and highly fashionable enclave. Property prices illustrate the change in Kinnerton Street's social status; when this scene was photographed, a six room house could be rented for £40 per annum.

Belgrave Square, *c.* 1904. Belgrave Square, one of the grandest of the great London squares, was built from 1827, mostly to the designs of George Basevi. Belgrave Square's illustrious former residents include a list of English aristocracy too long to mention here, but the houses are now embassies or offices.

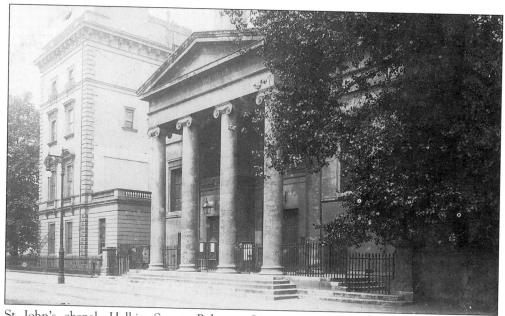

St John's chapel, Halkin Street, Belgrave Square, *c.* 1906. This presbyterian chapel's architecture complemented that of neighbouring Belgrave Square, but by 1907 it had gone, with a large red brick private house taking the site. This was occupied from 1946 by the Caledonian Club, which had previously held a number of addresses in the West End since its foundation in 1897.

Wilton Row, April 1963. A few yards distant, but world away from the thunderous traffic of Knightsbridge and Hyde Park Corner, is a network of cobbled mews and picturesque culs-de-sac where an almost rural atmosphere prevails in the middle of the town. The Grenadier, a colourful mews pub, can be found in Wilton Row, still with its sentry box and, apparently, a ghost of a guards officer who was caught cheating at cards and flogged to death. Wilton Row was called Wilton Crescent Mews until 1937.

Hyde Park Corner station, Knightsbridge, c. 1914. This was the original Hyde Park Corner station on the Great Northern, Piccadilly, and Brompton Railway – now the Piccadilly line – which opened for business on 15 December 1906. The old station had lifts down to platform level, but when the booking hall was replaced by a subterranean complex on 23 May 1932, new escalators took over their job. The street level entrance was then closed, but it can still be seen fulfiling a new role as a pizza restaurant. Felix Sartori's Park View Hotel occupied the building's upper floors, with a foyer on the ground floor, and a restaurant on the mezzanine, enjoying a fine view of Hyde Park. A railway poster at the station entrance rashly promises the traveller that it was 'Underground to Anywhere'.

Knightsbridge from Wilton Place, *c.* 1904. Almost all the buildings in this Edwardian view have been rebuilt; those to the right being replaced by the Berkeley Hotel, which moved here from Piccadilly in 1972, and a small cinema, The Minema, which opened on 12 May 1973. Further along, a flag was flying from the Alexandra Hotel, the site of which has been rebuilt twice during this century. Shops to the left were swept away with road widening in the 1960s for the construction of the Hyde Park Underpass.

Knightsbridge, by Albert Gate, *c.* 1904. Two grand mansions, built by Thomas Cubitt in 1845, flank the entrance to Hyde Park at Albert Gate. Beyond the French Embassy, old Trinity chapel and neighbouring shops were replaced in 1908 by Parkside, a large development of flats. This is the location of the original village of Knightsbridge, where the waters of the Westbourne stream flowed under a bridge on one of the principal roads from London to the west of England.

Knightsbridge from Brompton Road, c. 1904. The road junction is popularly known as 'Scotch Corner', after the well known stores, The Scotch House, which occupies the shops on the left. These were built from 1900-2 on the site of what was once Knightsbridge Green, originally a true village green, only a fragment of which survives. The grandiose Hyde Park Hotel, built in 1888, can be seen in the centre, and, to the right, work was in progress on Knightsbridge station, which opened on 15 December 1906. A remodelled Knightsbridge station opened on 18 February 1934, with entrances by Sloane Street and Hans Crescent.

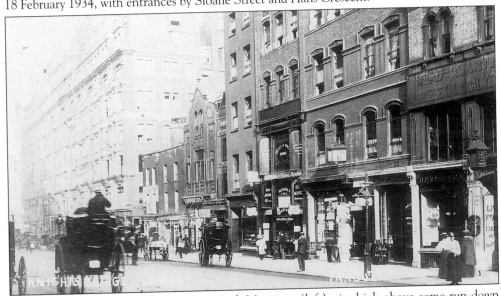

Knightsbridge, c. 1904. The impressive Park Mansions (left), rise high above some run-down property by Knightsbridge Green which was replaced by the Normandie Hotel in 1912. The small shops contained several restaurants, including the Coffee & Cocoa Room, and Pacifico de Maria's restaurant, where a pot of tea, roll and butter was available at the un-Knightsbridge-like price of 5d. To the right, the archway led into the tiny cul-de-sac, where the Rutland Yard riding school was ideally placed to give riding lessons in Hyde Park.

Raphael Street, Knightsbridge Green, *c.* 1905. This small street developed along the line of an old footpath through Knightsbridge's fields but, in Victorian times, it degenerated into a slum. The houses have all gone now, to be replaced by goods access and car parks for the postwar office developments of Brompton Road and Knightsbridge.

Montpelier Place, *c.* 1905. Development of the Montpelier streets began in 1826 on fields once owned by a wealthy Huguenot family, the Moreaus, whose name lives on in Moreau House, a modern building in Brompton Road. It was an unfashionable neighbourhood, but as is so often the case in London, the social status of an area can change, and the Montepeliers are now as smart an address as any.

Suffragette Band, Prince's skating rink, Hill Street (now Trevor Place), May 1909. Ladies of the Women's Social and Political Union, the Suffragettes, on parade during their exhibition and sale of work at Prince's Rink. Early in the century, the Suffragettes mounted a vigorous campaign for female voting rights, with street parades, demonstrations, and rallies in Hyde Park and Trafalgar Square. Prince's skating rink was a fashionable resort of society during the Edwardian era, when there was a craze for indoor skating, but the popularity of the rink declined, and it ended its days as a depot for Daimler Motors. A row of modern town houses stands here now.

The Women's exhibition and sale of work, Prince's rink, May 1909. The guiding light behind the highly successful Knightsbridge fund raising events was Sylvia, one of the Pankhurst sisters, whose artistic talents had been enhanced by her studies at the Royal College of Art in Exhibition Road. The exhibition brought together the skills of Suffragettes from many parts of the country, as this well laden stall demonstrates. The ladies' white dresses with purple and green trimmings, the Suffragette colours, were mirrored in miniature form on the doll that forms part of this exhibit.

Hyde Park Barracks, Knightsbridge, *c.* 1905. The first barracks were built for the Horse Guards in 1795, but were replaced by the buildings we see here in 1880. These in turn succumbed to the bulldozers, and an ultra-modern barracks designed by Sir Basil Spence arose on the site. Completed around 1970, the great central tower is a considerable, if controversial, landmark.

The South Carriage Drive, Hyde Park, 1903. The carriage drives of Hyde Park were a favourite meeting place and promenade for people of fashion, and were described in the 1890s as '...unbroken files of elegant equipages and high-bred horses in handsome trappings moving continually to and for, presided over by sleek coachmen and powdered lackeys, and occupied by some of the most beautiful and exquisitely dressed women in the world.' The photograph is of the scene near Hyde Park Corner, and shows several fine turn-outs of carriages and liveried coachmen in their top hats. There is also a motor-car sporting one of the new licence plates (A898), that had just been introduced.

Rotten Row, Hyde Park, c. 1922. Hyde Park's famous horse ride takes its name from 'Route du Roi', the King's Road from St James's Palace to Kensington Palace. Here we see a group of society children enjoying a ride in the park during the 1920s, much as they do today.

The Serpentine, Hyde Park, c. 1910. Hyde Park's history dates back to the time of Henry VIII, who enclosed the abbey lands of the manor of Hyde, and created a deer park. The park's lake, the Serpentine, was formed in 1730 at the instigation of Queen Caroline, who was anxious that the park's muddy stream, the Westbourne, should be transformed into a spectacular water feature. This was done by damming the stream at its eastern end, seen here, with surplus waters escaping over a pretty waterfall into a lower pool (The Dell), and thence underground to the Thames. Modern tea rooms now occupy this corner, but the Serpentine's teeming wild life is still an attraction for the young.

Brompton Higher Grade National School, Montpelier Street, c. 1903. This early-nineteenth-century school, complete with bell-cote, stood at the corner of Cheval Place, (once called Chapel Place), on part of the boundary between the boroughs of Kensington and Westminster. It was originally the Old Brompton chapel, but Montpelier Galleries, the head office of Bonham's auction house is here now.

This magnificent beast, the property of the City of Westminster works department, is seen around 1920 as Princes Gardens acquires a new road surface. Following war damage, most the Victorian houses of Princes Gardens were replaced by the new buildings of Imperial College.

Three
Mayfair and St James's

Mayfair, like Belgravia, has been an aristocratic quarter of London since it was first built up with elegant terraces and squares of town houses, and the grand mansions of the nobility. At its heart is Shepherd Market, and old-world network of narrow streets and passages crammed with shops and restaurants. This was built around 1746 by Edward Shepherd on the site of a notorious and riotous annual fair once held on the fields here during May. Although this view is over ninety years old, the essential character of Shepherd Market remains, even though its trendy pavement cafes impart a rather continental air nowdays.

Shepherd Market, c. 1904. Edwardian Shepherd Market was a considerable shopping centre supplying the every day needs of Mayfair's residents. George Hayward's ironmongery shop (left), had a wide ranging stock from the pots and pails piled up on the pavement, to petrol and oil for the car. To the right was the Curzon Registry Office for servants above the shop of George Copsey, hairdresser. The road then had a cobble-stone surface, and the buildings had East Anglian style pantile roofs, now rare in central London.

Market Street, c. 1907. This was one of Alfred Starley's trio of shops in Shepherd Market, with a rather unhygienic looking display of fish in the open air. Starley's other shops traded in poultry and cheese.

Shepherd Market, c. 1904. Another view in Shepherd Market, bustling with the everyday activities of shoppers and shopkeepers, who then included Charles Cowley, dairyman, seen on the right with milk churns ready for local deliveries. The projecting corner of East Chapel Street, Trebeck Street since the 1930s, can be seen in the centre of picture.

Shepherd Street, by Hertford Street, c. 1905. Although most of the old buildings of Shepherd Market still stand, these shops have been replaced by a huge block of flats, Carrington House. A tiny covered entrance, seen behind the horse, led to a cul-de-sac, whose name, Ducking Pond Mews, recalled Mayfair's rustic past when duck hunting with dogs was commonplace. King Charles II is rumoured to have been present at some of these gatherings to view the sport.

Shepherd Market, *c.* 1950. The village character of Shepherd Market was still apparent in this view from the 1950s, when there was time for a gossip by the market stalls, although the dog doesn't look pleased at being photographed. The newsgents shop (left), advertises a familiar publication of yesteryear, *Picture Post.*

Dover Street Studios, *c.* 1908. 'The Dover Street Studios offer to advertise the service of more than seventy of Britain's prettiest women for showcards, catalogue, and poster photographs, which will call attention to the goods you sell. All models are exclusive, and at short notice, Living Pictures, telling the advertiser's story, can be photographed in the well-known "Dover Street Style"…'. So runs the text of this photographic advertising card, with an Edwardian lady enticingly demonstrating that the use of a pretty girl to promote a product is not a new idea. The studios were at 38, Dover Street.

Down Street, 1924. The street was laid out in the 1720s, and takes its name from the bricklayer, John Downes. To the left was Down Street station, one of London's 'lost' underground stations. This Piccadilly line station opened on 15 March 1907 and closed on 21 May 1932. The British Empire Exhibition at Wembley was in progress when this photograph was taken, and a return ticket from Down Street to the exhibition cost 2/9d. Part of Christ church, built in 1865, is in the background.

Dover Street from Piccadilly, c. 1912. To the right was another Piccadilly line station that will not be found on a modern map, Dover Street (St James's), this being the original name of Green Park station. The name changed on 18 September 1933 for the opening of the rebuilt station, when new escalators replaced the old lifts.

Piccadilly, *c.* 1903. Piccadilly is Mayfair's southern boundary, where these old stone fronted mansions still look out over Green Park. The exception was the brick built house by Park Lane (now Old Park Lane), once the home of Lord Elgin, and where the Elgin Marbles were kept when first brought to this country from Greece. Closed, shuttered, and awaiting demolition, the house was replaced in 1904 by a remarkable building in green and white stone, which since 1971 has been a place of pilgrimage for rock music fans worldwide, the Hard Rock Cafe. To the left, a water cart lays the dust of an Edwardian summer, where the eastern portals of Hyde Park underpass now are.

Piccadilly and Green Park, *c.* 1910. A melée of late Edwardian traffic passes some of Piccadilly's old balconied houses by Bolton Street, with the familiar bulk of the Ritz, dating from 1906, on the right.

Park Lane and Dorchester House (left), *c.* 1904. Dorchester House was one of the grand mansions for which Park Lane was once noted, and with its Italian Palazzo design in Portland stone and famed marble staircase, was as magnificent as any of them. It was built in 1851 for the Holford family, but its magnificence did not save it from the demolition gangs, and by 1930, it had gone, to be replaced by an ultra-modern hotel, the Dorchester. The houses to the right, actually backs of houses in Seamore Place, were demolished in 1937 for a road scheme that created a new entrance to Park Lane from Curzon Street. A grey 1960s office block has replaced the old houses, centre of picture.

The Dorchester Hotel, 1930. The elegance of the new Dorchester Hotel, built to the designs of W. Curtis Green, had yet to emerge from the builder's scaffolding, but a large painting of the revolutionary new hotel was on display to hint at the splendours to come.

Park Lane by Hertford Street, and Pitts Head Mews, *c.* 1904. There could hardly be a greater contrast between these aristocratic old town houses and the building that replaced them in 1963, the London Hilton Hotel, with its thirty floors towering aggressively above the streets of Mayfair. The terrace to the left was once part of Seamore Place, and still exists up to the point where Curzon Street was cut through in 1937. The Poet's Fountain, complete with statues of Milton, Chaucer and Shakespeare was erected in 1875, but removed after the Second World War.

LONDON. Park Lane. No. 1154.

Park Lane, by Upper Grosvenor Street, *c.* 1920. These bow-windowed Regency houses were more in the style of a Sussex seaside town than of London, but they were particularly suitable for this location to get the best of the views over Hyde Park. The houses on the left still stand in a fine state of preservation but those beyond Upper Grosvenor Street were replaced in 1927 by the massive Grosvenor House Hotel.

60

GROSVENOR HOUSE. LONDON.

FK.1579.

Grosvenor House, *c.* 1904. Grosvenor House, the London mansion of the Dukes of Westminster, was designed by Thomas Cundy and built in 1842. The great Corinthian colonnade was modelled on Trajan's Forum in Rome, and the long south-facing terrace led down to an extensive garden that bordered Park Lane. The house and grounds were eventually sold to Lord Leverhulme and, by 1928, it had gone the way of the majority of Park Lane's mansions, and was replaced by the Grosvenor House Hotel.

Grosvenor Square, *c.* 1904. Mayfair's largest square was laid out in 1725 by Sir Richard Grosvenor, and through the decades was as fashionable an address as any, with most of the houses being occupied by people of title. The present century has seen the rich variety of the square's old houses replaced by a more unified neo-Georgian style, except on the western side, where a more revolutionary building has housed the Embassy of the United States of America since 1961.

61

Park Street from Upper Grosvenor Street, *c.* 1904. The sight of these rather dowdy shops and carriage works may well surprise anyone familiar with the elegant and exclusive Park Street we know today. To the left at No. 41 was Henry Massey's stationery shop, established in 1776, and beyond a boot makers, at No. 45a, there was a hairdressers, and Mrs Ann Hutton's bakery at the corner of King Street Mews, now Culross Street. T. Peters & Sons, the coachbuilders, occupied the further King Street Mews corner. None of these buildings were to survive for much longer, as flamboyant private mansions took their sites.

South Audley Street by Grosvenor Square, *c.* 1904. The 'Georgianisation' of Grosvenor Square's southern side also removed these old buildings, with their intricate first floor ironwork, and shops which included Edward Langlois's Librarie Anglo-Francaise, and the Dancock family dairy. One of Dancock's milk-carts is seen outside their shop in readiness for a delivery. Clients would have brought their own jugs to fill from the tap in the churn.

South Audley Street from South Street, *c.* 1904. One of Mayfair's unchanged street-scapes still has the same occupant of the large shop to the right, Thomas Goode, the china and glass merchants. Grosvenor chapel (centre), was built around 1730.

Farm Street, *c.* 1903. This is another street whose name recalls Mayfair's rural past, in this case, the Hay Hill Farm of the seventeenth century. The glory of Farm Street is the Roman Catholic church of the Immaculate Conception, opened on 31 July 1849, extended gradually through the decades, and seen here before a new outer aisle and chapels had been added early in the century. These were built on the site of the old mews house seen next to the church. The unassuming exterior gives little indication of the architectural riches within, which have made Farm Street church a favourite venue for society weddings. In 1903, Farm Street was still a working mews, with the premises of Charles Bonnett, jobmaster, to the left of the church, and a small side turning, Archibald Mews, where there were 'suites of stabling' to let. Mayfair telephone exchange was built on the site of the mews houses, but the Punchbowl pub still stands, usefully placed to provide a pre-nuptial fortifier for the church's latterday bridegrooms. The photographer has captured an earlier clientele, with a line of carts, each with a minder, as their drivers avail themselves of the good cheer dispensed by landlady, Mrs Fanny Rees. The cart on the left belonged to local fruiterers, Ambrose & Co. of Mount Street.

Hayes Mews, *c.* 1912. This was another humble byway, with coaches and horses stabled on the ground floor, and the coachmen and their families living upstairs. Fortunes have changed, however, and these are now very desirable homes, although some have been rebuilt. There is a very rare survival at the far end of Hayes Mews facing Waverton Street, in the form of an eighteenth-century weatherboarded house with its upper floors overhanging the pavement.

Davies Mews, *c.* 1912. Davies Mews is now taken up with the extensive antique galleries of 'Grays-in-the-Mews', but it was all very different early in the century when Henry Rosoman had his livery stables at Nos 1 to 4, before diversifying into the heavy removal business.

Berkeley Square, *c.* 1904. Berkeley Square is famous for its nightingale, and notable for its towering plane trees, but much of the old glamour and elegance of this eighteenth-century square vanished during the 1930s and 1950s, as massive commercial buildings replaced blocks of early houses. The view is of the south eastern corner of the square, where attractive turn-of-the-century houses still stand by Hay Hill. The solitary shop was that of Sharpe & Hale, the librarians, while, to the right, the trees spread out from the garden of old Lansdowne House, built by Robert Adam in 1784 for the Marquess of Bute, who never occupied it.

Berkeley Square by Bruton Street, *c.* 1920. The fading gentility of these eighteenth-century houses was replaced in 1937 by the brashly modern Berkeley Square House, which swallowed up much of the square's eastern side, together with part of Bruton Street, including the house where HM The Queen was born on 21 April 1926.

Davies Street by Mount Row, *c.* 1904. Davies Street was remarkable for the length of its cab stand, which extended along the middle of the road for most of its length. The old houses typified the style of Mayfair's early developments, but their uncompromisingly modern replacements could be from anywhere.

Davies Street from Bourton Street, *c.* 1904. Some of the eighteenth-century buildings that once stood here, with St George's public baths and wash-houses mid-way along the terrace. All, apart from Bourdon House, right, have been rebuilt during this century. Claridges Hotel, a favourite with visiting royalty, can be seen in the distance.

C.M. Davies Cambrian Dining Rooms and Davies Hotel, Avery Row, *c.* 1908. A charming corner of eighteenth century Mayfair that lasted until around 1910, when it was replaced by Avery Row House. A village atmosphere still pervades the narrow streets hereabouts, built close to what is now one of London's subterranean rivers, the Tyburn brook.

Old Bond Street and New Bond Street, *c.* 1903. The history of one of Britain's most exclusive shopping streets began in 1684, when the financier Sir Thomas Bond acquired building leases on what was then known as Albermarle Ground, little knowing that his name was to live on as a byword for luxury shopping. The view looks north towards Bruton Street, where the slight valley of the Tyburn brook, which once flowed through open fields, may be detected.

Old Bond Street by Grafton Street, *c.* 1920. A sunny day in the early 'twenties brought out several parasols, as the ladies promenade by Bond Street's jewellery and dress shops, with a discreet branch of Boots, the chemist in the midst of them. The Hansom cabs of the Edwardian view had given way to motor cabs, and the traffic was busy enough to require a policeman on point duty. Advertising banners were in vogue then, as they are today.

New Burlington Street provides the backdrop for three Napier cars, pictured in 1903. The cars had been specially prepared to compete for the Gordon Bennett Trophy, the races for which took place in Ireland in 1903. New Burlington Street runs from Savile Row to Regent Street, (seen in the background), and was built on the Burlington Estate from the 1730s.

The urbane image of Savile Row, the internationally renowned centre of gentleman's tailoring, was temporarily in ruins, along with some of its buildings on 16 September 1940, when a high-explosive bomb destroyed Nos 7 and 8, and left the top floor of No. 6 hanging precariously. When first built during the 1730s, Savile Row was a fashionable residential street, and was to attract a number of famous residents, including Sheridan, the dramatist, and architects S.P. Cockerell and George Basevi.

Regent Street by Conduit Street, *c.* 1904. The building of Regent Street was one of London's most ambitious examples of town planning of the early nineteenth century, with a scheme designed by John Nash to create a new road linking Carlton House, the palace of the Prince Regent, with Marylebone Park, now Regents Park. The new road was finished in 1820, and soon became fashionable, with bright new paint applied to the terraces annually. By the beginning of the twentieth century, Regent Street was looking its age and, although the shops were as smart as ever, some additions and alterations at roof level were giving the road a rather untidy look, as we can see in this photograph. With the new century, there were great changes ahead for Regent Street, and we can see the first of them here in the form of Regent House, whose grander style gradually led to the demise of Nash's stuccoed terraces.

Regent Street by Vigo Street, *c.* 1905. Although not as aristocratic as Bond Street, the variety and quality of Regent Street's shops has made it one of London's most popular shopping streets. Three out of the four shops nearest to the camera enjoyed royal patronage, including: Scott Adie, purveyors of Scotch woollen and tartan hosiery on the Vigo Street corner; Eugene Rimmel, the perfumers at No. 119; and Abraham Marx, the jewellers at No. 121.

Regent House, Regent Street, *c.* 1905. The scale of the new Regent Street when compared with the old is well caught in this view, with Regent House, built 1899, rising above the old Nash terraces. Prominent on the Hanover Street corner was Verrey's restaurant, with smaller shops leading to a long vanished department store, Jay's Ltd, the costumiers, who held Royal Warrants from Queen Victoria and Queen Alexandra. The shop extended from Princes Street to Oxford Circus.

Lyons tea shop, Piccadilly, 20 September 1934. Until recent years, Lyons corner houses and tea shops were as familiar a sight in London as McDonald's restaurants are today, and, with their high standards of catering and value for money, were just as popular. The first Lyons tea shop opened in 1894 at 213, Piccadilly, and to celebrate the fortieth anniversary in 1934, the waitresses, popularly known as 'nippies', were dressed up in the Victorian uniforms of their predecessors.

Piccadilly, by St James's Street, c. 1905. This is the boundary between Mayfair and St James's, and shows Burlington House, home since 1868 of the Royal Academy of Arts. Just out of sight is St James Piccadilly, a Wren church built from 1676-84, and, close by, was the Egyptian Hall, which pioneered the display of motion pictures, (or 'animated photographs' as they called them), in 1896. The building works in progress here, show some of the wooden scaffolding then in use.

St James's Street, c. 1904. St James's Street was laid out in 1670, and extends from Piccadilly to St James's Palace, which was the official residence of the monarch from the time of William III to the accession of Queen Victoria, in 1837. The view is of the corner by King Street, which was soon to be rebuilt in the heavier style of the new Regent Street.

St James's Theatre, from Bury Street, c. 1904. This beautiful theatre was built in 1835, and under the management of Mr (later Sir) George Alexander staged for the first time Oscar Wilde's *The Importance of Being Earnest*, and *Lady Windermere's Fan*. Closure of the theatre in 1957 was followed by controversial demolition in 1959, the site then being used as an office block, St James's House, itself replaced by a new St James's House in 1989.

Crown Court, c. 1904. This narrow passageway close to St James's Palace remains much as it was in this Edwardian photograph – narrow, busy, and illuminated by gas lamps. Early in the century there were butchers, a hairdressers, grocer, cheesemonger, bootmaker and a rag and bottle dealer all trading here, together with a laundry and a tailor. Its picturesque pub, the Red Lion, still exists and is advertised as 'London's last village inn'. In dark, narrow streets like this, mirrors were angled to reflect daylight into otherwise gloomy rooms.

St James's Place, c. 1904. There are still quiet side roads like this, just off the busy St James's Street, where the surviving eighteenth-century houses have large bay windows in an effort to catch a glimpse of Green Park. A wall plaque at No. 4 records that Chopin left the house to give his last public performance at Guildhall in 1848 just before his death. Sir Francis Chichester, the celebrated yachtsman, lived at No. 9 St James's Place.

St James's Square, c. 1904. Planning began around 1662 for this, the oldest of the West End squares, when Henry Jermyn, Earl of St Albans, acquired building rights on part of St James's Field, close to St James's Palace. It has throughout its history, been the abode of the of the aristocracy and of a number of the gentleman's clubs for which the area is still noted. This view shows the north and west sides of the square, with Chatham House on the York Street (now Duke of York Street) corner. Three Prime Ministers have lived at Chatham House: William Pitt, the Earl of Derby and William Ewart Gladstone. The fine classical façade, centre, belongs to Litchfield House, built 1764 and the grand Victorian mansion next door houses the East India and Sports Club.

Bury Street, c. 1905. This is another street dating from the early development of St James's by the Earl of St Albans during the 1670s. Many of the houses contained bachelor's apartments and, in 1928, the Quaglino brothers founded Quaglino's Restaurant, which soon became a favourite with high society. Many fine-art dealers have made this part of town a centre for their galleries.

Duke Street, c. 1906. There were 'chambers to let' at Charles Godson's apartment house, left, in a street where there were numerous similar establishments. Part of the premises of Spinks & Sons, dealers in coins, banknotes and medals now occupies the site.

United Service Club, Waterloo Place, *c.* 1903. One of the great West End gentleman's clubs, the United Service Club was founded in 1817, and moved to its grandiose new building in 1828. This was designed by John Nash at the southern end of his Regent Street scheme, but was remodelled by the club's own architect, Decimus Burton, who famously designed the screen at Hyde Park Corner. The club closed in 1976, and the building now houses the Institute of Directors.

Waterloo Place and Pall Mall, *c.* 1903. This dates from 1816, and was named after the battle that had taken place one year earlier. By 1899, the old buildings on the eastern side of Waterloo Place were overshadowed by the stone-fronted Carlton Hotel, and eventually these too were rebuilt on a similar scale. The Carlton Hotel was demolished in 1957, but a fragment of old Pall Mall remains at Royal Opera Arcade, London's oldest shopping arcade, dating from 1816-18. In Edwardian days, it was remarkable for the number of bootmakers who traded there. In 1807, Pall Mall became the first London street to be lit by gas.

Four
Soho and Theatreland

Fouberts Place, c. 1904. Soho is unique, a cosmopolitan village at the heart of London's West End, with a tradition of foreign occupancy stretching back to the 1670s, when Huguenot immigrants settled in the new streets, then being laid out on the former St Giles Field. The view of Fouberts Place, which runs from Regent Street to Marshall Street, typifies an enduring Soho street-scape which then included Rudolph Modrack's hairdressing saloon in a rare (for central London) weatherboarded building. A modest 6d would have bought a 'cut from the joint and two vegetables' at the Oriental pub on the corner of Kingly Street while, further along, a host of small shops served the needs of this populous quarter. The street was named after Solomon de Foubert, one of the Huguenot settlers, who went on to found a riding school nearby.

Kingly Street, c. 1906. Another lively scene in the busy streets of west Soho with, to the left, Evan Davis's ironmongery store on the Fouberts Place corner. The Oriental is on the opposite corner, where an inflationary 8d 'cut from the joint' had been added to the menu. The street's original name, King Street, was changed to Kingly Street in 1906.

Fouberts Place from Regent Street, c. 1908. This part of Fouberts Place was swept away during the rebuilding of Regent Street and, although the passageway survives, the old shops, which include those of John Cridlan, butchers (left), and Fouberts Place post office (right), have all gone. There was a tantalising display of illustrated books in the window of Hamley Bros bookshop, in what was an early manifestation of a now familiar name, Hamleys Ltd., the vast toy emporium in Regent Street.

Fouberts Place from Great Marlborough and Carnaby Streets, *c.* 1905. To the right was the Shakespeare's Head pub, established around 1735 and since rebuilt. Refreshment was also available at Kohler's Dining Rooms and, further along, a haircut cost 4d at Rudolph Modrack's barber shop. Porteous Gillhespy, the outfitters on the Carnaby Street corner (left), were holding their summer sale, little realising that sixty years hence, the street would become a world famous centre of teenage fashion.

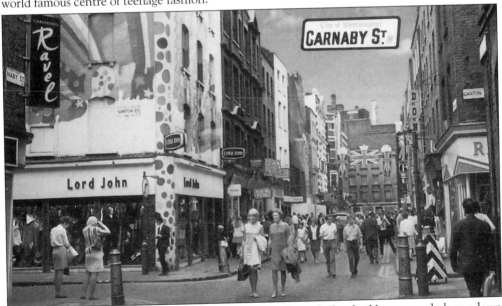

Carnaby Street, *c.* 1966. The 'Swinging Sixties' transformed what had become a drab, rundown back street into an internationally renowned centre for colourful boutiques, where the trendy young flocked to acquire their 'gear' in a blaze of Union Jacks and psychedelia. The photograph pre-dates Carnaby Street's pedestrianisation, and the laying of a unique multi-coloured road surface, since replaced by more restrained brick surfacing.

Glasshouse Street looking towards Piccadilly Circus, *c.* 1905. Frenchman Daniel Thévenon established his cafe-restaurant, the Café Royal, here in 1865, and it soon became a notable meeting place for writers and artists, including Oscar Wilde, Whistler, Aubrey Beardsley and Augustus John. The Café Royal was rebuilt from 1923-28, with its main entrance in Regent Street. The vast Regent Palace Hotel, built 1912-15, took the sites of the old buildings on the left, where Sherwood Street may be seen. The canopy of the Café Monico in Piccadilly Circus is visible in the distance.

Glasshouse Street by Air Street, *c.* 1905. There is now a pizza restaurant in place of Mash & Austin's fruit and vegetable shop, and their neighbour, Rick's Dairy in Air Street (right), is nothing more than a distant memory. Warwick Street and Brewer Street are to the left of the picture.

Brewer Street and Glasshouse Street, c. 1905. The Bodega Company's Spanish wine cellars stood on this prominent corner, in a building now occupied by the Glassblower pub. The view looks along Brewer Street, which still had its old shops before they were replaced by the Regent Palace Hotel's new building from 1912. The Warwick Street corner (left), shows one of the attractive street name signs of this area, with the name made up with individual tiled letters set into the brickwork.

Brewer Street, 1912. The preparation of the site for the Regent Palace Hotel involved excavations on a vast scale, which became even more extensive as part of Brewer Street subsided into the workings. The view is looking westwards, with anxious business owners, including those of Cowderoy, Bland & Co., billiard table manufacturers, and W. Truman, jeweller standing by, doubtless wondering whether the abyss would also claim their premises. Mercifully, it did not, and the buildings still stand, with the Regent Palace now dominating the view to the left in spite of the earlier mishaps.

Little Pulteney Street from Great Windmill Street, c. 1900. This street has lost its market stalls, its name (it was added to Brewer Street in the 1930s) and its sober Victorian image, for it now forms part of Soho's colourful neon-lit entertainment and night life quarter. Most of the buildings still stand, however, with the flats of St James's residences above the shops that once included Otto Mathias' newsagents (right), and a good selection of useful domestic stores and old family businesses, some of which are still here. Long gone, though, are a branch of Lilley & Skinner on the Greens Court corner, and two pubs, the Luke's Head and the Queens Head (left). The tiny opening at the far left led to William & Mary Yard, where Brewer Street garage now stands.

Denman Street, c. 1912. This was Villars House, where there were 'furnished bedrooms for gentlemen' behind the luxuriant window boxes. The building still stands, but with its open basement paved over, and a betting shop on the ground floor.

The Royal Ear Hospital, Dean Street, c. 1910. An impromptu tea party above the teeming streets of Soho for these jolly nurses, as Matron pours the tea. The hospital was established in Dean Street in 1816, moved to Frith Street in 1876, and returned to Dean Street in 1904.

The Red Lion, Great Windmill Street, c. 1923. Mrs Harriet Rees was landlady at the Red Lion, which still stands and has changed little externally, on the corner of Archer Street. The street was named after a windmill that stood nearby during the seventeenth century when the area was being built up. The Windmill Theatre stands close to the pub, and was the only London theatre to remain open throughout the Second World War, with its popular French style non-stop variety show *Revuedeville*, which had been introduced in 1932.

Macclesfield Street, *c.* 1908. A scene outside the premises of Staveley & Co., the shipping agents and continental carriers on the Dansey Place corner. The well-laden wagon contained a consignment of band instruments crated up in readiness for the first stage of their journey to Kabul, where they were to be received by the King of Afghanistan. Macclesfield Street lost many of its original houses during the construction of Shaftesbury Avenue (right), which opened in 1886.

Public call office, Gerrard Street, from Macclesfield Street, *c.* 1905. Before the standardised street telephone kiosk was introduced around 1921, it was necessary for everyone who did not have a receiver to patronise a public call office, or premises which displayed the once familiar sign 'telephone calls may be made from here', usually accompanied by the bell logo of the National Telephone Company. The larger offices like Gerrard Street were open for twenty-four hours every day, and international calls could be made. In post-war years, the rather undistinguished Gerrard Street area has been transformed into one of London's most remarkable neighbourhoods, for it has become the capital's Chinatown, and the streets are now filled with the sights, sounds, and aromas of the Orient.

The cutting of Shaftesbury Avenue through a network of populous Soho streets during the 1880s gave the area a fine new street, which became remarkable for the number of theatres and cinemas along its length. A stone in the wall of the London Pavilion (right), commemorates the 'laying of the first stone in the new street' on 8 June 1885. The Monico Restaurant (left), has been rebuilt in recent years, and the London Pavilion redeveloped, behind its preserved façades, as a shopping centre which was opened by Prime Minister Margaret Thatcher, on 22 July 1988.

The London School of Motoring, c. 1906. In a city where, for centuries, the horse had ruled the road, the complexities of the new-fangled motor car brought the needs for new skills to be learnt, for those who could afford it. The London School of Motoring, Shaftesbury Avenue, was on hand to teach the art of driving, maintain machinery, and coax a reluctant engine into life. It was to be another thirty years before the compulsory driving test was introduced. This busy scene was at the company's garage, off Tottenham Court Road.

Berwick Street, *c.* 1908. Another of the busy narrow streets of Soho, this one enlivened by its traditional street market. The view is to the south, with old buildings on the left, many of which still stand. To the right, everything has gone, including St Luke's church, and the neighbouring White Bear, all replaced in 1959 by Kemp House, a seventeen-storey block of flats. In the distance are Peter Street and Walkers Court, now the frenetic heart of Soho's racy red-light district.

Berwick Street Market, *c.* 1908. Berwick Street remains narrow, congested, and full of street cries and market characters, much as it was when this scene, complete with rather unhygienic fish stall (left), was captured on camera.

The Florence Hotel and Restaurant, Rupert Street, *c.* 1907. Soho has traditionally been home to a remarkably varied selection of foreign restaurants and cafes, a fine example of which was Luigi Azario's well staffed Florence Restaurant. This card was sent by a new member of staff who writes: 'You will see by this card what a big place I am at, I like it very much, but London does not suit me'. For many, Soho is an acquired taste!

Mario Coda's hairdressing saloon, 33 Old Compton Street, *c.* 1925. A full range of products was available at Mario Coda'a saloon, where the window display reveals the ideals of feminine beauty of the day. These included a rather tortured permanent wave, and the fearsome assembly of rollers needed to achieve the style.

Old Compton Street from Dean Street, c. 1908. Old Compton Street is regarded as the 'High Street' of Soho but, with its concentration of foreign restaurants and international businesses, is quite unlike any other High Street in Britain. This Edwardian postcard reveals the multi-national flavour of the area with Librarie Parisienne, the newagents at No. 48, followed by Au Petit Riche, and the premises of Samuel Wenter, trunk manufacturer. There was also Dieppe Restaurant and, to the right, the shop of Percy Denny, the Anglo-French outfitters, which can still be found on the corner. The postcard was published by Libreria Española of Charing Cross Road, and sent to Paris.

Old Compton Street from Wardour Street, c. 1900. The south side of Old Compton Street is seen on the right, with the Swiss Hotel, then under the management of Horace Caleb Phipps, rising above the eighteenth-century terrace. The old houses have been rebuilt with only the Swiss Hotel (now 'Comptons of Soho') surviving, but minus its tall gables. We can only wonder at the activities of the youth pictured face down across the pavement (right), while another looks on.

Messrs Plume and Parry stand at the door of their ironmongery shop at 47 Old Compton Street, around 1910. The firm also specialised in footware, and were manufacturers of the boot trees and lasts used during shoe repair. The building's style was typical of Soho's eighteenth-century architecture, but this one has been replaced by a small modern block of flats and shops.

MAISON JOSEPH, 24, Bateman Street, Soho, W. I. J. JANSEN.

THE FOOD FOR CHAMPION DOGS AND CATS.

Maison Joseph horsemeat shop, Bateman Street, by Greek Street, c. 1925. Soho is famed for its specialist food stores, and Joseph Jansen's emporium was one of many that catered for minority tastes. Horsemeat was sold here for human consumption, as well as for pet food.

Weddes Hotel, Greek Street, from Bateman Street, c. 1905. This fine Georgian building housed Josiah Wedgewood's London's showrooms from 1774 until 1795, and his name lives on in Wedgewood Mews, the yard that at the time of this photograph housed William Latchford, the timber merchant. The shop on the left is the same one as in the photograph above – in this earlier view, it was Alphonse Dugeno's bicycle shop.

Piccadilly Circus, *c.* 1921. Piccadilly Circus, or Regent Circus South as it was originally called, came into being with the construction of Regent Street from 1816 to 1829. When first built, the scale of Piccadilly Circus was roughly that of the Oxford Circus we know today, but while Oxford Circus (Regent Circus North) has retained its shape, Piccadilly Circus has been rebuilt and enlarged at various times throughout its history. The Shaftesbury Memorial Fountain (Eros) was unveiled in 1893, adding a new focal point as Piccadilly Circus gradually developed into one of the worlds great meeting places, with its shops, theatres, restaurants, cockney flower girls, and eventually, bright lights. The photograph has caught the last of the old Regency buildings of Regent Street, including the County Fire Office, rebuilt in 1924. To the right, the advertising lights were spreading across the frontage beside Shaftesbury Avenue and Glasshouse Street, with *The Times* newspaper advertising 'free motor insurance' for its readers. Traffic lights had yet to arrive, and a lull in the busy traffic gave the two policemen on point duty a moment to chat.

The lights of Piccadilly Circus, c. 1923. Piccadilly Circus's famous illuminated signs made a modest debut during the 1890s, but it was not until after the First World War that the lights became one of London's more popular attractions, adding excitement and colour to the city's entertainment district. The most elaborate lights have traditionally covered Piccadilly Mansions and adjacent frontages (left), where the Bovril and Schweppes signs made an early appearance. The London Pavilion (centre and right) has also put on a good show through the decades, and here we see a floodlit poster in addition to the other lights, which in those days were comprised of individual electric bulbs; the neon lights came later. The London Pavilion then carried the sign 'The Centre of the World', a reflection of Piccadilly's status as the world's favourite meeting place.

Leicester Square and the Alhambra, c. 1923. To the east, Leicester Square shone nearly as brightly, especially by Cranbourn Street, left. The east side of Leicester Square was dominated from 1854 by the Alhambra theatre, an exuberantly Moorish creation with its pair of minarets. The Alhambra undertook a variety of roles throughout its life, including music hall, circus, variety theatre, and it also staged ballet and promenade concerts. Blondin, the tightrope walker of Niagara fame, appeared here, as did George Robey. Demolition in 1936 robbed London of a fine building, but the Odeon cinema was an equally eye catching replacement from 2 November 1937.

Leicester Square, *c.* 1904. Leicester Square was laid out from the 1670s on an area known as Leicester Fields. Its fine houses attracted numerous aristocratic residents, together with writers and artists including Hogarth and Joshua Reynolds. The square began to lose its residential character during the mid-nineteenth century, as theatres, Turkish baths and hotels moved in. The view is from the east side of the square, showing the Alhambra and Charles Bartholomew's Turkish baths ('the largest in the London') next door. Oscar Phillippe's Cavour Hotel was another of the district's foreign hotels, in a building that is still recognisable, although it is now a Mexican restaurant. There are many continental style pavement cafes here now, in the attractive pedestrian precinct.

The Quick Service Cafeteria, Leicester Square, *c.* 1935. This restaurant displays the bright modernistic style of the 1930s, with its neon signs, and a good meal of roast beef or Irish stew available at a mouth-watering 1/6d. There were also after-theatre snacks, and that favourite of London's West End, oysters.

The Leicester Square bookstall, Green Street, c. 1906. A fine display by Robert Willis 'Stationer and Postcard Specialist' at his shop, off Leicester Square. Posters for sporting and motoring publications were well represented here, with *The Car* offering articles on: Monaco Fortnight; 'a new motor bus'; auto cycle clubs, and motor mountaineering, while the *Motor Car Journal* refers to 'Brighton Police Traps'. A poster for the *London Opinion* intriguingly refers to 'Jerome K. Jerome and the Lady Typist'. The post card section of the shop (right), has attracted several gentleman who were admiring a window-full of Edwardian actresses.

Jean Barrière's Librairie Centrale at 17 Green Street had a good selection of 'newspapers of the world' at the shop, advertised as 'un coin de France en Angleterre' – a corner of France in England. Green Steet was later renamed Irving Street in memory of Sir Henry Irving, the first knight of the theatre. The street now forms part of the Leicester Square pedestrian precinct, with a continental atmosphere enhanced by the attractive open air cafes and restaurants.

Charing Cross Road and Wyndhams theatre, 1909. Charing Cross Road, famous for its bookshops and theatres, was constructed during the 1880s along the line of the former Castle Street and Porter Street. Wyndams theatre was built in 1889, and is seen here during a revival of the ever popular *Brewster's Millions*. Leicester Square station (left of the theatre), opened on 15 December 1906, and is pictured before an office block was built above the station during the 1920s. To the left is part of Sandringham Buildings, whose impressive canyon-like walls once lined both sides of Charing Cross Road. The flats date from 1884, when they were built to house some 900 people displaced by the development of Shaftesbury Avenue. The flats were opened by the Prince and Princess of Wales, (later King Edward VII and Queen Alexandra), but the western blocks were rebuilt in modern times. To the right is St Martins Court which, together with the neighbouring Cecil Court, make up a delightful area of narrow pedestrian streets lined with antiquarian and theatrical bookshops, and other specialist businesses.

St Martins Lane and Coliseum theatre, c. 1905. St Martins Lane is a street of sixteenth-century origin, and was the principal north/south thoroughfare hereabouts before Charing Cross Road was built. The Coliseum was built in 1904 as a variety theatre – Ellen Terry and Sarah Bernhardt appeared here. The building was used as a cinema at various times, and became the home of the English National Opera, once known as the Sadlers Wells Opera Company, from 1968. The ornate lamp of the former Trafalgar pub is seen to the left.

Trafalgar Square, c. 1920. Trafalgar Square was laid out in the 1820s and, with its famous buildings, fountains, monuments, and flocks of greedy pigeons, has become another of London's great meeting places. Morleys Hotel of 1831 vintage (right), lent a touch of Regency elegance to the east of the square until its site was taken for South Africa House, built in 1935. Also visible is the church of St Martin-in-the-Fields, whose history goes back to 1222, with the present church dating from 1722-26. The tiny circular construction topped by a gas-lamp (left), was a police station – not surprisingly, it was Britain's smallest.

Strand, Charing Cross, c. 1920. Part of Morleys Hotel and Charing Cross post office is on the left, with the Grand Hotel on the right, dating from 1878. The latter has been reconstructed with its shops set back to form a covered walkway. The buildings from Craven Street to Charing Cross station have all been replaced in modern times.

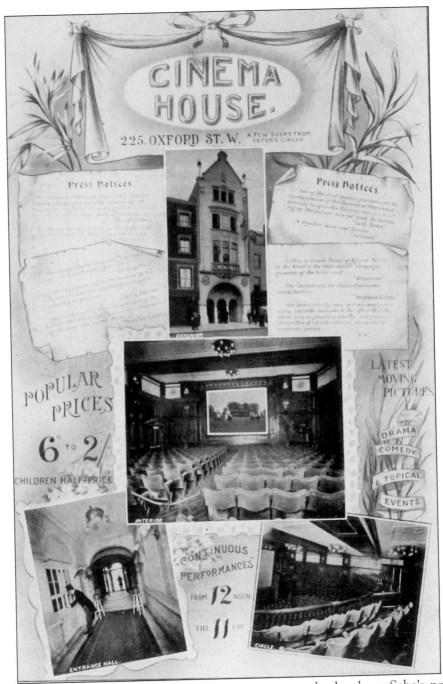

Cinema House, Oxford Street, c. 1910. This cinema was a landmark on Soho's northern boundary from its opening on 14 July 1910 to closure on 8 December 1984, by which time it had become the familiar multi-screen complex, Studios 1, 2, 3, and 4. Early cinema going was relatively expensive, with a seat in the Circle costing 2/-, but there was a Jacobean style oak panelled auditorium to give a touch of Edwardian luxury. The cinema retained the tall, narrow frontage throughout its life, and in later years made a dramatic show with an intricate display of neon lighting.

Fairyland, Tottenham Court Road, *c.* 1910. Amusement arcades played their part in the range of diversions offered by the West End's entertainment district, and although this one fell just outside Westminster's boundaries, it was a typical example. Fairyland was owned by Henry Standon Morley's Automatic Exhibitions, and among the delights provided were the 'Monorail Adventure Skittle Alley', and measuring machine for weight and height at $\frac{1}{2}$d a time. Madame Pauline offered 'good sound advice' on the first floor, with 'revolver gunshooting' in the rifle range on the top floor.

Covent Garden, *c.* 1906. This area was laid out in the seventeenth century on land that had, in the Middle Ages, been a produce garden of Westminster Abbey. The famous fruit and vegetable market began in a modest way around 1656, but it was not until 1828 that the familiar market was built to the designs of Charles Fowler. The market moved away to Nine Elms in 1974, leaving the old buildings to be adapted for a variety of modern uses, including antique and craft markets, trendy restaurants, the Theatre museum, and the London Transport museum (right). Street musicians and entertainers have moved in to display their talents, with the actor's church, St Pauls (by Inigo Jones, 1631), providing a suitably theatrical backdrop.

Costermonger, Covent Garden, *c.* 1910. Costermongers came to Covent Garden from all over London to purchase produce for their barrows. Nowadays, it is London's visitors who find much to attract them here, with exhibitions, events, and sometimes a fair, all adding to this neighbourhood's bustling street life. The old road surface, with its time-worn granite setts, has been preserved.

Ticket queue, Royal Opera House, Covent Garden, *c.* 1910. This queue makes itself as comfortable as possible, with portable seats and something to read while waiting for tickets for the opera. To the right we see several representatives of a long lost London tribe, the District Messenger boys, with their uniforms and pill box hats worn at a jaunty angle. One of their duties was to queue for tickets for those unable or unwilling to do it themselves. The Opera House opened in 1858, and was the third on the site, the first two having burnt down.

Midnight at a Salvation Army soup kitchen, *c.* 1904. Practical help, as well as spiritual ministration was on hand for the homeless in this once deprived corner of Westminster, as a queue for free soup makes its way slowly towards the Salvation Army's food and shelter depot in Stanhope Street. To the right was the disused Olympic theatre, where, following closure in 1899, evangelistic services were organised by the St Giles Christian Mission. Much of this old neighbourhood disappeared following the opening, in 1905, of the new Aldwych/Kingsway road scheme.

Wych Street, *c.* 1892. One of London's first major road schemes of the twentieth century was the construction of Kingsway and Aldwych through a slummy area of old narrow streets that included Newcastle Street, Holywell Street, and Wych Street, an eastern extension of Drury Lane. Wych Street contained a number of ancient timber-framed houses that overhung the roadway, like the Rising Sun pub, seen here.

Aldwych, c. 1912. The new Aldwych quickly established itself as an important part of London's road network, with the build up of traffic by 1912 demanding a policeman on point duty by the Strand. The Gaiety theatre (right) was built in 1903 and replaced the old Gaiety which had stood in the Strand until displaced by the new roads. The Waldorf hotel (left) was built in 1907.

Aldwych, c. 1925. The twin theatres, Waldorf and Aldwych, with the Waldorf Hotel sandwiched between them, make an impressive sight on the western part of the Aldwych crescent. The corner with Kingsway (right), can be a windy one, as may be seen here as the *Evening Standard* newspaper seller struggles to retain his placards and his hat.

Five

A Westminster Miscellany

Queen Anne Mansions and Broadway, c. 1905. Queen Victoria is said to have been far from amused when the upper windows of what was for the time (the 1870s), an exceptionally tall block of flats began to peek cheekily over the more genteel rooftops towards Buckingham Palace. Some decades later, Sir Nikolaus Pevsner described the black barrack block walls as 'that irredeemable horror', but it was all demolished in 1972, and replaced by the towering concrete of the Home Office. To the left was the St James's Tavern and an entrance to St James's Park underground station, which opened on 24 December 1868 on a site now dominated by the imposing headquarters of London Transport, 55 Broadway. This was designed by Charles Holden, the architect of a number of London's underground stations, and opened in 1929, with shopping arcades, and a new station entrance. Queen Anne's Gate, one of Westminster's finest early-eighteenth-century streets, lies behind the buildings on the right.

Horse-bus, Charing Cross Road, *c.* 1908. The reliable, if old fashioned, horse drawn buses were the mainstay of Westminster's road transport in the first decade of the twentieth century, but by the end of August 1914, they had all been replaced by increasingly efficient motor buses. This Hammersmith bound specimen was photographed in Charing Cross Road, by New Oxford Street, at a spot now occupied by the fountains in front of one of London's more controversial tower blocks, Centre Point.

Motor-bus, Charing Cross Road, 1903. Progress in applying the new technology of the motor car to provide London with a motor-bus service was painfully slow, with a number of experimental vehicles being tried with varying degrees of failure. This is one of them, an American Fischer bus powered by a mixture of electric batteries and petrol, pictured on a trial run in Charing Cross Road by the Garrick theatre. The vehicle was briefly owned by the London General Omnibus Company.

The Royal Standard music hall, *c.* 1903. The Royal Standard, originally Moy's music hall, was the oldest building in London to have a music hall licence. It was replaced in 1911 by the Victoria Palace theatre, where in later years the theatre played host to *The Crazy Gang* and *The Black and White Minstrel Show*. The celebrated Russian ballerina, Anna Pavlova, famously made her London debut here, and to commemorate the occasion, a statue of her was added to the theatre's frontage.

Victoria Street, *c.* 1920. By its proximity to Victoria station, and with a variety of transport interchanges and hotels, this continues to be an area busy with travellers and visitors to London. The photograph pre-dates the building of an office block above Victoria underground station (right). Beyond the distant rooftops is the 284 ft campanile of Westminster's Roman Catholic cathedral, built from 1895-1903 on the site of the old Westminster Bridewell (prison). To the left is the more modest tower of the Victoria Palace theatre.

City of Westminster street watering cart, *c.* 1905. The street watering cart performed an essential service during dry weather, when the unmade roads of London turned unpleasantly dusty. This cart, No. 2, is pictured in Buckingham Palace Road opposite the premises of May Bros., the hosiers on the Palace Street corner.

Gorringe's delivery van, *c.* 1906. Frederick Gorringe's store occupied a large block of buildings in Buckingham Palace Road, and was apparently a favourite with the ladies of Queen Victoria's household at Buckingham Palace. The delivery van on its rounds, proudly displays the Royal Warrant. The store was founded in 1858 but closed during the 1960s.

Victoria Street, c. 1906. Victoria Street was created as another of the nineteenth-century town planning schemes with the dual object of improving the city's road system and sweeping away areas of run-down housing. While the new street did not have the elegance of the earlier Regent Street, it was, nevertheless, lined with impressively solid Victorian blocks, including the Army & Navy Stores (right). This shop did not have the usual window displays for its merchandise and was only available to members of the services and their families until 1918, when everyone was finally allowed in. The traditional window displays followed and, in 1926, experimental apparatus, an early step in the development of television, was demonstrated in public there for the first time by its inventor, John Logie Baird. Victoria Street has been almost entirely rebuilt since the Second World War; only the Albert pub (left) and Artillery Mansions (centre) have resisted the bulldozers. Beyond the Albert pub, part of one of London's more eccentric lost buildings may have been seen – the Hotel Windsor, a creation of such elephantine ugliness that its replacement by a banal office block has left London the poorer.

Christ church, Victoria Street, *c.* 1923. This is one of Westminster's lost churches, built in 1841-43 to a design by Ambrose Poynter, and demolished in 1954. The site has been left undeveloped, apart from the garden that offers a welcome green oasis along the solidly built-up Victoria Street.

Strutton Ground from Greycoat Place, *c.* 1903. The popularity of this old fashioned street market remains undiminished as it bustles away serving local residents and office workers. Although many of the shops have been rebuilt, the newer buildings are on a similar scale, preserving the flavour of the street. Older residents may remember the Army & Navy cinema, which was built on the site of Mrs Shuttleworth's Dining Rooms at No. 30. The cinema opened in 1913, and had become a dance hall by 1931, but no trace of either establishment remains. The view is part of a series published in France by a photographer who, judging by the caption, appears to have lost his way.

The London County Council fire station, Greycoat Place, *c.* 1906. This building opened on 22 May 1906 and was brand new when photographed, having just replaced the old fire station in Francis Street. Some very dilapidated property may be seen to the right by Strutton Ground and Great Peter Street.

Westminster Cathedral Catholic procession, Greycoat Place, from Rochester Row, *c.* 1910. Religious processions like this were commonplace during the early part of the century, and often attracted crowds to view the spectacle. The fire station is seen in the background, but with a then much tidier Strutton Ground corner adjoining it.

Rochester Row and St Stephens church, c. 1905. This picture gives a graphic reminder of some of the very poor property that still existed in Westminster early in the century. This grimy row of tiny shops ran from Allen Street (now Vane Street) to Vincent Square but, for all their modest aspect, they contained many useful shops for the local community, including those of Alexander Kieff, confectioner; John Reed, newsagent; and Joseph Sandford, fried fish. The most distant shop was that of Frederick Clifford, bird dealer, while the third from the right contained Frederick Dorney, zinc worker. His premises are easily spotted by a pair of ventilation pipes, which would not have improved the air quality upstairs. J. Whitehead & Sons, the undertakers on the Allen Street corner, looks suitably grim. The shops were replaced in 1913 by a hostel for Kings College hospital, and the Empire Hospital for Paying Patients. The Rochester Hotel is here now. On the left, a lamp marks the premises of Thomas Cocks & Sons, carriage-masters and undertakers. St Stephens church was built from 1847-49 in stone brought from Northumberland, giving the church an impressively dark, northern look.

George Blackwell's shop, Rochester Row, *c.* 1906. Feline heaven was to be found at No. 27 Rochester Row (part of the terrace pictured on the preceding page) where George Blackwell, 'the noted pussy's butcher' had his emporium. The cat's meat man was once a familiar sight in the streets of London, with his barrow or basket filled with strips of horse-meat on sticks.

Jas. Wilson's shop, Rochester Row, *c.* 1912. The grandly named *Westminster Museum* on the Emery Hill Street corner looked a fascinating place with its displays of collectables, including a fearsome array of swords, guns and knives, together with some attractive ceramics. The main business was picture-framing.

Page Street, *c.* 1906. By the 1920s, the Page Street and Vincent Street area had degenerated into an overcrowded slum, but by the end of the decade, everything had been cleared away, and a fine new estate of flats built. These were distinguished by their checkerboard brick and plaster decorations, and were designed by Sir Edwin Lutyens, the English architect whose earlier work had included Hampstead Garden Suburb, and the Cenotaph in Whitehall. The view shows Esher Street (centre), and the more distant Kensington Place, where the Grosvenor Arms pub occupied a corner. The cottages on the left were of the most basic design, with their doors opening straight onto the pavement, where we see a lady occupant of one of them enjoying a doorstep gossip.

Horseferry Road, c. 1906. The road takes its name from the ancient ferry that until the nineteenth century transported horses across the Thames to Lambeth. Although most of the road has been rebuilt, a little of the old property remains, including part of this terrace by Arneway Street with a pub at either end. The Barley Mow pub, originally with fine etched glass windows, has been rebuilt, and work began on a new Westminster Baptist church, here in 1934.

Horseferry Road, by Monck Street, c. 1906. Behind this elegant façade lay the historic works which, during the early nineteenth century, brought gas lighting to London for the first time. The gas was manufactured from coal brought along the Thames to Millbank, and thence in wagons to the works, where the malodorous processes did little for the quality of life locally. The whole of the site is now covered by the monstrous two hundred foot high horror blocks of the Department of the Environment, built in 1963-71 – merciful early demolition of these has been promised. The building line (right) was considerably set back with the building of Great Westminster House in 1937, itself replaced now by a new block, Great Minster.

Horseferry Road, 1902. It is difficult to believe that the splendid city-scape at the Millbank end of Horseferry Road, with its noble pre-war office buildings, can ever have looked like this during the twentieth century, but as we see here, it did. This was part of the notoriously slummy Millbank area which was progressively cleared after the First World War. These old houses had grim basement rooms that were plagued by damp and the ever present threat of flooding from the Thames, which became a terrifying reality in January 1928, when the river burst its banks, drowning a number of people. The side turning in the centre of this view, bore one of Westminster's least elegant names, Grub Street. Old Lambeth Bridge is just visible in the distance. (Greater London Record Office).

Marsham Street, c. 1904. Richard Morgan's Marsham dairy brought an almost rural touch to Marsham Street with 'cows kept on the premises', for Mr Morgan was a licenced cow keeper. He is pictured here with his staff, delivery cart, and under the archway leading to the yard, one of his beasts. This site is now covered by the Ninth Church of Christ, Scientist, built from 1926-30.

Thames House, and Imperial Chemical House, c. 1932. The stately new Millbank rises above the derelict ruins of the old, as roofless terraces and cleared sites await their new buildings, which included, in 1939, a new Westminster hospital. Horseferry Road, Marsham Street, and Page Street with its arched entrance from Millbank can be seen here, as can the new Lambeth Bridge which had just opened. The four corner towers of St Johns church, Smith Square, are visible to the right.

32 — LONDON. — Lambeth Bridge.

Old Lambeth Bridge, c. 1904. Built as a replacement for the old ferry and opened on 10 December 1862, this was the ugliest of the Thames road bridges, and the least effective, with a carriageway wide enough for just two wagons. It was also the weakest and any wagon that ventured onto the bridge's tottering spans had to pass fierce signs warning that 'All vehicles must cross at a walking pace'. By the time it had closed, the bridge had weakened to such an extent that only pedestrians were permitted to use it. A fine new bridge was opened by King George V on 19 July 1932.

Millbank and Horseferry Road from Lambeth Bridge, 1902. The squalor of old Millbank has been well caught by this photograph, which makes an interesting comparison with the aerial view from the 1930s on page 117. There can be few people who remember a pub and a row of shops on Millbank, but here we see Charles Springthorpe's Brown Bear pub on the Horseferry Road corner, with an adjoining terrace of shops, which included those of James Condy, dairyman and Alex Fitzgerald, oil and colourman. His shop was on the corner of Romney Street, which no longer has a junction with Millbank. The old shops looked across a very narrow roadway to the riverside wharves, which then included Horseferry Wharf, close to Lambeth Bridge. Victoria Tower Gardens stand there now. (Greater London Record Office).

Champions Alley, Millbank, 1902. This humblest of byways was entered through a narrow archway under one of Horseferry Road's houses, and ran into the now defunct Millbank end of Romney Street, beneath the Ship pub. Narrow, insanitary courts like this were once commonplace in the poorest parts of London, but have now all but vanished. (Greater London Record Office).

York Buildings, Grub Street, Millbank, 1902. This wretched group of hovels was obviously no longer fit for human habitation, even in this very deprived quarter, and are seen here in use by costermongers for storage. An attempt had been made at some time to brighten the gloom with a coat of whitewash, and some of the walls still show the fittings that once held the washing lines strung across the court. (Greater London Record Office).

The Houses of Parliament and Westminster Bridge from Lambeth Bridge, c. 1903. One of Westminster's most famous and familiar views looked very different at the beginning of the century, when the riverside commercialism of Millbank ran right up to the Palace Of Westminster, the Houses of Parliament. The picturesque jumble of sailing barges, wharves and factories which included the London Hydraulic Power Company's pumping station; the Westminster Electric Supply Corporation; the Hovis Bread Flour Co.; and the Dorset, Union and Horseferry wharves, were cleared away for the Victoria Tower Gardens, which were laid out in 1912. Part of the gardens were constructed on land reclaimed from the Thames, with a new river wall continuing the line set by the terrace of the Houses of Parliament, seen here projecting well out into the river. Now, the great plane trees of Victoria Tower Gardens act as a perfect foil to the gothic magnificence of Sir Charles Barry's Palace of Westminster, the foundation stone of which was laid in 1839, with the building mostly completed in 1860.

Millbank Street and Abingdon Street, *c.* 1862. At the time of this historic view, the new Houses of Parliament were one of London's latest wonders, a fairytale gothic palace by the Thames that replaced the ancient buildings burnt down on 16 October 1834. To the right, beside the long forgotten Chequers pub, was the monumental Victoria Tower, then the largest square tower in the world, which had been completed only two years earlier. In the centre of the photograph is Old Palace Yard, overlooked by the great window of Westminster Hall. This venerable building was originally built by William Rufus from 1097, was remodelled in 1397, survived the fire of 1834 and is Britain's largest Norman hall. To the left, the houses of Abingdon Street survived until the 1940s, and were eventually replaced by Abingdon Street Gardens, a place well known to viewers of television news, for it is here that many interviews with MPs take place against a backdrop of Parliament's long façade.

The Houses of Parliament from St Margaret's churchyard, *c.* 1862. The gothic stone tracery by St Stephen's entrance to the Houses of Parliament rises behind the classical Law Courts, an eighteenth-century building which then obscured the St Margaret Street façade of Westminster Hall. The Law Courts moved to their spectacular new home in the Strand in 1882, and the redundant Westminster building was then demolished. To the right is part of Westminster Abbey's King Henry VII chapel, dating from 1503.

Westminster Abbey from the Thames, *c.* 1906. Work is in progress on the clearance of the old Millbank wharves, which was beginning to open up a new vista of Westminster Abbey rising above the chimney pots of Abingdon Street. A new landmark in the shape of the Church Commissioner's headquarters had arrived in 1903 (centre) but the old Hovis building was still standing and the muddy Thames foreshore was still awaiting reclamation and a river wall to accommodate Victoria Tower Gardens

Westminster Abbey, 1911. Over a 1000 years of English history are encapsulated in the venerable Abbey, where the alterations and additions of past centuries are on view for all to see. Kings and Queens have been crowned here since the time of Edward the Confessor in the eleventh century and, in this view, we see the elaborate annexe specially erected for the coronation of King George V in 1911. The annexe temporarily obscured the main entrance to the Abbey but the lower part of the towers added by Nicholas Hawksmore in the late 1730s, are seen beyond it.

A London fog, *c.* 1910. London once had a reputation as a foggy city, with countless chimneys pouring out clouds of acrid smoke, blackening the walls of buildings and the lungs of inhabitants. In times of cold anticyclonic weather, the smoke would be trapped close to the ground in a choking sepia-coloured cloud which would bring London to a halt for days at a time. Such a day is pictured here, with the statue of Queen Boadicea outlined against a tram on Westminster Bridge, while Big Ben, on the other side of the road, is lost in the murk. The man with the telescope by the Boadicea statue, who charged a penny for a look at Big Ben, would not have done good business on this day. This is one of the atmospheric images created by the master of the genre, Fred Judge. (Judges of Hastings).

A London frost, *c.* 1903. In previous centuries, it was not unusual for the wide sluggish Thames to freeze during periods of sustained frost, and for frost fairs to be set up on the ice, with ox-roasting, sales booths and other revelry. As more land was reclaimed from the river, and the muddy banks replaced by the embankments, the river's flow became faster, and ice was rarely seen, apart from during the most severe weather, as here, when this arctic scene was photographed by Waterloo Bridge.

Pavement artist, Victoria Embankment, *c.* 1905. The pavement artist is one of London's most enduring street characters, with eye-catching displays of varying degrees of talent. Victoria Embankment is one of the traditional locations for these gentlemen, and here we see a range of pictures on display, and chalk drawings on the paving slabs, together with the traditional hat to lighten the pocket of the passer by.

Kingsway tram subway, Victoria Embankment, *c.* 1908. Besides improving London's road system, the new Kingsway/Aldwych development gave the city its unique tram subway, which extended from Kingsway to Victoria Embankment, with a subterranean station along the way. It partly opened on 24 February 1906, and was fully in operation on 10 April 1908, when single deck trams ran right through the tunnel for the first time. Double deckers came later, and lasted until the night of 5/6 April 1952, when the tunnel was closed. Part of it was converted into the Strand Underpass, which opened to road traffic on 21 January, 1964.

A wet night, Victoria Embankment from the Kingsway subway, c. 1920. Bad weather can give London its own kind of beauty, particularly by the Thames, where the effect of mist and rain have attracted generations of artists and photographers. Here, the tram lines glisten, and a policeman stands in a dripping cape against a backdrop of electric trams on their special reserved tracks by the river. 'Beware Cars Crossing' is one of London's vanished street signs, and referred to the tram-cars which ran along the Embankment until the night of 5/6 July 1952.

Victoria Embankment and Waterloo Bridge from Hotel Cecil, c. 1923. The majestic sweep of the Thames is well caught from this unusual viewpoint high above the Embankment. Old Waterloo Bridge was opened on 18 June 1817 and, after part of it subsided during the 1920s, it was replaced by the sleek, streamlined structure we know today, whose formal opening was delayed by the Second World War until 10 December 1945. The Savoy Hotel (left) opened in 1889, and was remodelled in 1910, while Hotel Cecil gave its site in 1931 for Shell-Mex House. The background is of the City of London, its skyline then still dominated by St Pauls Cathedral and the City churches.

126

Essex Stairs tea room, Milford Lane, *c.* 1928. One of the joys of London are its hidden corners, quaint survivals from earlier centuries in the midst of the modern city. This old-world nook, with its pretty tea room, lay between the thundering traffic of the Strand and Victoria Embankment.

Milford Lane and Essex Stairs, *c.* 1920. This lane runs along part of Westminster's boundary with the City of London, and still retains much of its old fashioned charm. Although rebuilt, the arched entrance to Essex Street is still there, together with Essex Stairs, which led directly to the waters of the Thames at high tide before the Embankment was built. Here, an old chap in a bowler hat entertains passers by with his mouth organ, by the walls of the Temple.

Building the Victoria Embankment, *c.* 1864. Somerset House provided the view point for this historic image, which vividly illustrates the scale of the land reclamation from the Thames that preceded construction of Victoria Embankment from 1864-70. The man responsible for this massive project, which included a new sewerage system, was the Metropolitan Board of Works Engineer, Sir Joseph Bazalgette. The work also included the construction of the District Railway extension from Westminster Bridge to Blackfriars beneath the new roadway. Temple station (then called 'The Temple'), opened on 30 May 1870 near the centre of this view. Visible here are some bow-windowed properties of the old riverfront (far left) and the works of Gwynne & Co., the engineers, whose walls had previously been lapped by the waters of the Thames. Beyond was Milford Lane, and over the City of London boundary, Middle Temple library with its patterned roof. This was built in 1858 and demolished during the 1880s. Further on were the gas-holders of the City of London gasworks, with St Pauls Cathedral rising high above them. To the right, old Blackfriars Bridge is seen in the last year of its life. The foundation stone of the new bridge was laid by the Lord Mayor of London on 20 July 1865.